I

There is a line among the fragments of the Greek poet Archilochus which says: 'The fox knows many things, but the hedgehog knows one big thing.'* Scholars have differed about the correct interpretation of these dark words, which may mean no more than that the fox, for all his cunning, is defeated by the hedgehog's one defence. But, taken figuratively, the words can be made to yield a sense in which they mark one of the deepest differences which divide writers and thinkers, and, it may be, human beings in general. For there exists a great chasm between those, on one side, who relate everything to a single central vision, one system, less or more coherent or articulate, in terms of which they understand, think and feel – a single, universal, organising principle in terms of which alone all that they are and say has significance – and, on the other side, those who pursue many ends, often unrelated and even contradictory, connected, if at all, only in some *de facto* way, for

---

* Archilochus fragment 201 in M. L. West (ed.), *Iambi et Elegi Graeci*, vol. 1 (Oxford, 1971).

some psychological or physiological cause, related by no moral or aesthetic principle. These last lead lives, perform acts and entertain ideas that are centrifugal rather than centripetal; their thought is scattered or diffused, moving on many levels, seizing upon the essence of a vast variety of experiences and objects for what they are in themselves, without, consciously or unconsciously, seeking to fit them into, or exclude them from, any one unchanging, all-embracing, sometimes self-contradictory and incomplete, at times fanatical, unitary inner vision. The first kind of intellectual and artistic personality belongs to the hedgehogs, the second to the foxes; and without insisting on a rigid classification, we may, without too much fear of contradiction, say that, in this sense, Dante belongs to the first category, Shakespeare to the second; Plato, Lucretius, Pascal, Hegel, Dostoevsky, Nietzsche, Ibsen, Proust are, in varying degrees, hedgehogs; Herodotus, Aristotle, Montaigne, Erasmus, Molière, Goethe, Pushkin, Balzac, Joyce are foxes.

Of course, like all over-simple classifications of this type, the dichotomy becomes, if pressed, artificial, scholastic and ultimately absurd. But if it is not an aid to serious criticism, neither should it be rejected as being merely superficial or frivolous; like all distinctions which embody any degree of truth, it offers a point of

Tolstoy and History

Taken from
The Hedgehog and The Fox

ISAIAH BERLIN

A Phoenix Paperback

This abridged edition, published in 1996 by Phoenix, contains pages 3 to
43, 80 and 81 of the 1992 edition of *The Hedgehog and The Fox*
first published in 1953 by Weidenfeld & Nicolson
A division of Orion Books Ltd
Orion House, 5 Upper Saint Martin's Lane, London WC2H 9EA

Cover illustration: Portrait of Leo Nikolaivitch Tolstoi, taken in the year
before his death, 1909; © Hulton Deutsch Collection

ISBN 1 85799 523 6

Typeset by Deltatype Ltd, Ellesmere Port, Cheshire
Printed in England by Clays Ltd, St Ives plc

view from which to look and compare, a starting-point for genuine investigation. Thus we have no doubt about the violence of the contrast between Pushkin and Dostoevsky; and Dostoevsky's celebrated speech about Pushkin has, for all its eloquence and depth of feeling, seldom been considered by any perceptive reader to cast light on the genius of Pushkin, but rather on that of Dostoevsky himself, precisely because it perversely represents Pushkin – an arch-fox, the greatest in the nineteenth century – as being similar to Dostoevsky, who is nothing if not a hedgehog; and thereby transforms, indeed distorts, Pushkin into a dedicated prophet, a bearer of a single, universal message which was indeed the centre of Dostoevsky's own universe, but exceedingly remote from the many varied provinces of Pushkin's protean genius. Indeed, it would not be absurd to say that Russian literature is spanned by these gigantic figures – at one pole Pushkin, at the other Dostoevsky; and that the characteristics of other Russian writers can, by those who find it useful or enjoyable to ask that kind of question, to some degree be determined in relation to these great opposites. To ask of Gogol, Turgenev, Chekhov, Blok how they stand in relation to Pushkin and to Dostoevsky leads – or, at any rate, has led – to fruitful and illuminating criticism. But when we come to Count Lev Nikolaevich Tolstoy, and ask this of him – ask whether he belongs to the first category or the second, whether he is a monist or a pluralist, whether his vision is of one or of many, whether he is of a single substance or compounded of heterogeneous elements – there is no clear or immediate answer. The question does not, somehow, seem wholly appropriate; it seems to breed more darkness than it dispels. Yet it is not lack of information that makes us pause: Tolstoy has told us more about himself and his views and attitudes than any other Russian, more, almost, than any other European writer; nor can his art be called obscure in any normal sense: his universe has no dark corners, his stories are luminous with the light of day; he has explained them and himself, and argued about them and the methods by which they are constructed, more articulately and with greater force and sanity and lucidity than any other writer. Is he a fox or a hedgehog? What are we to say? Why is the answer so curiously difficult to find? Does he resemble Shakespeare or Pushkin more than Dante or Dostoevsky? Or is he wholly unlike either, and is the question therefore unanswerable because it is absurd? What is the mysterious obstacle with which our enquiry seems faced?

I do not propose in this essay to formulate a reply to this question, since this would involve nothing less than a critical examination of the art and thought of Tolstoy as a whole. I shall confine myself to suggesting that the difficulty may be, at least in part, due to the fact that Tolstoy was himself not unaware of the problem, and did his best to falsify the answer. The hypothesis I wish to offer is that Tolstoy was by nature a fox, but believed in being a hedgehog; that his gifts and achievement are one thing, and his beliefs, and consequently his interpretation of his own achievement, another; and that consequently his ideals have led him, and those whom his genius for persuasion has taken in, into a systematic misinterpretation of what he and others were doing or should be doing. No one can complain that he has left his readers in any doubt as to what he thought about this topic: his views on this subject permeate all his discursive writings – diaries, recorded *obiter dicta*, autobiographical essays and stories, social and religious tracts, literary criticism, letters to private and public correspondents. But the conflict between what he was and what he believed emerges nowhere so clearly as in his view of history, to which some of his most brilliant and most paradoxical pages are devoted.

This essay is an attempt to deal with his historical doctrines and to consider his motives for holding the views he holds. In short, it is an attempt to take Tolstoy's attitude to history as seriously as he himself meant his readers to take it, although for a somewhat different reason – for the light it casts on a single man of genius rather than on the fate of all mankind.

II

Tolstoy's philosophy of history has, on the whole, not obtained the attention which it deserves, whether as an intrinsically interesting view or as an occurrence in the history of ideas, or even as an element in the development of Tolstoy himself.* Those who have treated Tolstoy primarily as a novelist have at times looked upon the historical and philosophical passages scattered through *War and Peace* as so much perverse interruption of the narrative, as a regrettable liability to irrelevant digression characteristic of this great, but excessively opinionated, writer, a lop-sided, home-made metaphysic of small or no intrinsic interest, deeply inartistic and thoroughly foreign to the purpose and structure of the work of art as a whole. Turgenev, who

---

* For the purpose of this essay I propose to confine myself almost entirely to the explicit philosophy of history contained in *War and Peace*, and to ignore, for example, *Sebastopol Stories*, *The Cossacks*, the fragments of the unpublished novel on the Decembrists, and Tolstoy's own scattered reflections on the subject except in so far as they bear on views expressed in *War and Peace*.

found Tolstoy's personality and art antipathetic, although in later years he freely and generously acknowledged his genius as a writer, led the attack. In letters to Pavel Annenkov,* Turgenev speaks of Tolstoy's 'charlatanism', of his historical disquisitions as 'farcical', as 'trickery' which takes in the unwary, injected by an 'autodidact' into his work as an inadequate substitute for genuine knowledge. He hastens to add that Tolstoy does, of course, make up for this by his marvellous artistic genius; and then accuses him of inventing 'a system which seems to solve everything very simply; as, for example, historical fatalism: he mounts his hobby-horse and is off! Only when he touches earth does he, like Antaeus, recover his true strength.'† The same note is sounded in the celebrated and touching invocation sent by Turgenev from his death-bed to his old friend and enemy, begging him to cast away his prophet's mantle and return to his true vocation – that of 'the great writer of the Russian land'.‡ Flaubert, despite his 'shouts of admiration' over passages of *War*

* See E. I. Bogoslovsky, *Turgenev o L. Tolstom* (Tiflis, 1894), p. 41; quoted by P. I. Biryukov, *L. N. Tolstoy* (Berlin, 1921), vol. 2, pp. 48–9.

† ibid.

‡ Letter to Tolstoy of 11 July 1883.

and Peace, is equally horrified: 'il se répète et il philosophise',* he writes in a letter to Turgenev, who had sent him the French version of the masterpiece then almost unknown outside Russia. In the same strain Belinsky's intimate friend and correspondent, the philosophical tea-merchant Vasily Botkin, who was well disposed to Tolstoy, writes to the poet Afanasy Fet:

> Literary specialists ... find that the intellectual element of the novel is very weak, the philosophy of history is trivial and superficial, the denial of the decisive influence of individual personalities on events is nothing but a lot of mystical subtlety, but apart from this the artistic gift of the author is beyond dispute – yesterday I gave a dinner and Tyutchev was here, and I am repeating what everybody said.†

Contemporary historians and military specialists, at least one of whom had himself fought in 1812,‡

---

* 'He repeats himself and he philosophises.' Gustave Flaubert, *Lettres inédites à Tourguéneff* (Monaco, 1946), p. 218.
† A. A. Fet, *Moi vospominaniya* (Moscow, 1890), part 2, p. 175.
‡ See the severe strictures of A. Vitmer, a very respectable military historian, in his *1812 god v 'Voine i mire'* (St Petersburg, 1869), and the tones of mounting indignation in the contemporary critical notices of A. S. Norov, A. P. Pyatkovsky and S. Navalikhin. The first served in the campaign of 1812 and, despite some errors

indignantly complained of inaccuracies of fact; and since then damning evidence has been adduced of falsification of historical detail by the author of *War and Peace*,* done apparently with deliberate intent, in full knowledge of the available original sources and in the known absence of any counter-evidence – falsification perpetrated, it seems, in the interests not so much of an artistic as of an 'ideological' purpose.

This consensus of historical and aesthetic criticism seems to have set the tone for nearly all later appraisals of the 'ideological' content of *War and Peace*. Shelgunov at least honoured it with a direct attack for its social quietism, which he called the 'philosophy of the swamp'; others for the most part either politely ignored it, or treated it as a characteristic aberration which they put down to a combination of the well-known Russian tendency to preach (and thereby ruin works of art) with the half-baked infatuation with general ideas character-istic of young intellectuals in countries remote from

---

of fact, makes criticisms of substance. The last two are, as literary critics, almost worthless, but they seem to have taken the trouble to verify some of the relevant facts.

* See V. B. Shklovsky, *Mater'yal i stil' v romane L'va Tolstogo 'Voina i mir'* (Moscow, 1928), *passim*, but particularly chapter 7. See below, pp. 40–1.

centres of civilisation. 'It is fortunate for us that the author is a better artist than thinker,' said the critic Dmitri Akhsharumov,* and for more than three-quarters of a century this sentiment has been echoed by most of the critics of Tolstoy, both Russian and foreign, both pre-revolutionary and Soviet, both 'reactionary' and 'progressive', by most of those who look on him primarily as a writer and an artist, and of those to whom he is a prophet and a teacher, or a martyr, or a social influence, or a sociological or psychological 'case'. Tolstoy's theory of history is of equally little interest to Vogüé and Merezhkovsky, to Stefan Zweig and Percy Lubbock, to Biryukov and E.J. Simmons, not to speak of lesser men. Historians of Russian thought† tend to label this aspect of Tolstoy as 'fatalism', and move on to the more interesting historical theories of Leontiev or Danilevsky. Critics endowed with more caution or humility do not go as far as this, but treat the 'philosophy' with nervous respect; even Derrick Leon, who treats Tolstoy's views of this period with greater care than the majority of his biographers, after giving a painstaking account of Tolstoy's reflections on the forces which dominate history, particularly of the

* *Razbor 'Voiny i mira'* (St Petersburg, 1868), pp. 1–4.
† e.g. Professors Ilin, Yakovenko, Zenkovsky and others.

second section of the long epilogue which follows the end of the narrative portion of *War and Peace*, proceeds to follow Aylmer Maude in making no attempt either to assess the theory or to relate it to the rest of Tolstoy's life or thought; and even so much as this is almost unique.*

* Honourable exceptions to this are provided by the writings of the Russian writers N. I. Kareev and B. M. Eikhenbaum, as well as those of the French scholars E. Haumant and Albert Sorel. Of monographs devoted to this subject I know of only two of any worth. The first, 'Filosofiya istorii L. N. Tolstogo', by V. N. Pertsev, in '*Voina i mir*': *sbornik pamyati L. M. Tolstogo*, ed. T. I. Polner and V. P. Obninsky (Moscow, 1912), after taking Tolstoy mildly to task for obscurities, exaggerations and inconsistencies, swiftly retreats into innocuous generalities. The other, 'Filosofiya istorii v romane L. N. Tolstogo, "Voina i mir" ', by M. M. Rubinshtein, in *Russkaya mysl'* (July 1911), pp. 78–103, is much more laboured, but in the end seems to me to establish nothing at all. (Very different is Arnold Bennett's judgement, of which I have learnt since writing this: 'The last part of the Epilogue is full of good ideas the johnny can't work out. And of course, in the phrase of critics, would have been better left out. So it would; only Tolstoy couldn't leave it out. It was what he wrote the book for.' *The Journals of Arnold Bennett*, ed. Newman Flower, 3 vols [London, 1932–3], vol. 2, 1911–21, p. 62.) As for the inevitable efforts to relate Tolstoy's historical views to those of various latter-day Marxists – Kautsky, Lenin, Stalin etc. – they belong to

Those, again, who are mainly interested in Tolstoy as a prophet and a teacher concentrate on the later doctrines of the master, held after his conversion, when he had ceased to regard himself primarily as a writer and had established himself as a teacher of mankind, an object of veneration and pilgrimage. Tolstoy's life is normally represented as falling into two distinct parts: first comes the author of immortal masterpieces, later the prophet of personal and social regeneration; first the aristocratic writer, the difficult, somewhat unapproachable, troubled novelist of genius; then the sage – dogmatic, perverse, exaggerated, but wielding a vast influence, particularly in his own country – a world institution of unique importance. From time to time attempts are made to trace his later period to its roots in his earlier phase, which is felt to be full of presentiments of the later life of self-renunciation; it is this later period which is regarded as important; there are philosophical, theological, ethical, psychological, political, economic studies of the later Tolstoy in all his aspects.

And yet there is surely a paradox here. Tolstoy's interest in history and the problem of historical truth was passionate, almost obsessive, both before and

the curiosities of politics or theology rather than to those of literature.

during the writing of *War and Peace*. No one who reads his journals and letters, or indeed *War and Peace* itself, can doubt that the author himself, at any rate, regarded this problem as the heart of the entire matter – the central issue round which the novel is built. 'Charlatanism', 'superficiality', 'intellectual feebleness' – surely Tolstoy is the last writer to whom these epithets seem applicable: bias, perversity, arrogance, perhaps; self-deception, lack of restraint, possibly; moral or spiritual inadequacy – of this he was better aware than his enemies; but failure of intellect, lack of critical power, a tendency to emptiness, liability to ride off on some patently absurd, superficial doctrine to the detriment of realistic description or analysis of life, infatuation with some fashionable theory which Botkin or Fet can easily see through, although Tolstoy, alas, cannot – these charges seem grotesquely unplausible. No man in his senses, during this century at any rate, would ever dream of denying Tolstoy's intellectual power, his appalling capacity to penetrate any conventional disguise, that corrosive scepticism in virtue of which Prince Vyazemsky invented for him the queer Russian term 'netovshchik'* ('negativist') – an early version of that nihilism

* See article by M. de Poulet in *Sankt-Peterburgskie vedomosti* (1869, No 144).

which Vogüé and Albert Sorel later quite naturally attribute to him. Something is surely amiss here: Tolstoy's violently unhistorical and indeed anti-historical rejection of all efforts to explain or justify human action or character in terms of social or individual growth, or 'roots' in the past; this side by side with an absorbed and lifelong interest in history, leading to artistic and philosophical results which provoked such queerly disparaging comments from ordinarily sane and sympathetic critics – surely there is something here which deserves attention.

III

Tolstoy's interest in history began early in his life. It seems to have arisen not from interest in the past as such, but from the desire to penetrate to first causes, to understand how and why things happen as they do and not otherwise, from discontent with those current explanations which do not explain, and leave the mind dissatisfied, from a tendency to doubt and place under suspicion and, if need be, reject whatever does not fully answer the question, to go to the root of every matter, at whatever cost. This remained Tolstoy's attitude throughout his entire life, and is scarcely a symptom either of 'trickery' or of 'superficiality'. With it went an incurable love of the concrete, the empirical, the verifiable, and an instinctive distrust of the abstract, the impalpable, the supernatural – in short an early tendency to a scientific and positivist approach, unfriendly to romanticism, abstract formulations, metaphysics. Always and in every situation he looked for 'hard' facts – for what could be grasped and verified by the normal intellect, uncorrupted by intricate theories divorced from tangible realities, or by other-worldly mysteries, theological, poetical and metaphysical alike. He was tormented by the ultimate problems which face young men in every generation – about good and evil, the origin and purpose of the universe and its inhabitants, the causes of all that happens; but the answers provided by theologians and metaphysicians struck him as absurd, if only because of the words in which they were formulated – words which bore no apparent reference to the everyday world of ordinary common sense to which he clung obstinately, even before he became aware of what he was doing, as being alone real. History, only history, only the sum of the concrete events in time and space – the sum of the actual experience of actual men and women in their relation to one another and to an actual three-dimensional, empirically experienced, physical environment – this alone contained the truth, the material out of which genuine answers – answers needing for their apprehension no special senses or faculties which normal human beings did not possess – might be constructed.

This, of course, was the spirit of empirical enquiry which animated the great anti-theological and anti-metaphysical thinkers of the eighteenth century, and Tolstoy's realism and inability to be taken in by shadows made him their natural disciple before he had learnt of their doctrines. Like M. Jourdain, he spoke prose long before he knew it, and remained an enemy of transcendentalism from the beginning to the end of his life. He grew up during the heyday of the Hegelian philosophy, which sought to explain all things in terms of historical development, but conceived this process as being ultimately not susceptible to the methods of empirical investigation. The historicism of his time doubtless influenced the young Tolstoy as it did all enquiring persons of his time; but the metaphysical content he rejected instinctively, and in one of his letters he described Hegel's writings as unintelligible gibberish interspersed with platitudes. History alone – the sum of empirically discoverable data – held the key to the mystery of why what happened happened as it did and not otherwise; and only history, consequently, could throw light on the fundamental ethical problems which obsessed him as they did every Russian thinker in the nineteenth century. What is to be done? How should one live? Why are we here? What must we be and do? The study of historical connections and the demand for empirical answers to these *proklyatye voprosy* ('accursed questions') became fused into one in Tolstoy's mind, as his early diaries and letters show very vividly.

In his early diaries we find references to his attempts to compare Catherine the Great's *Nakaz* – her instructions to her legislative experts – with the passages in Montesquieu on which she professed to have founded it.* He reads Hume and Thiers† as well as Rousseau, Sterne and Dickens.‡ He is obsessed by the thought that philosophical principles can only be understood in their concrete expression in history.§ 'To write the genuine history of present-day Europe: there is an aim for the whole of one's life.'** Or again: 'The leaves of a tree delight us more than the roots',†* with the implication

---

* L. N. Tolstoy, *Polnoe sobranie sochinenii*, ed. V. G. Chertkov (Moscow, 1934), vol. 46, pp. 4–28.

† ibid., pp. 97, 113, 114, 117, 123–4, 127.

‡ ibid., pp. 126, 127, 130, 132–4, 167, 176, 249; 82, 110; 140.

§ Diary entry for 11 June 1852.

** Entry for 22 September 1852.

†* N. N. Apostolov, *Lev Tolstoy nad stranitsami istorii* (Moscow, 1928), p. 20.

that this is nevertheless a superficial view of the world. But side by side with this there is the beginning of an acute sense of disappointment, a feeling that history, as it is written by historians, makes claims which it cannot satisfy, because like metaphysical philosophy it pretends to be something it is not – namely a science capable of arriving at conclusions which are certain. Since men cannot solve philosophical questions by the principles of reason they try to do so historically. But history is 'one of the most backward of sciences – a science which has lost its proper aim'.* The reason for this is that history will not, because it cannot, solve the great questions which have tormented men in every generation. In the course of seeking to answer these questions men accumulate a knowledge of facts as they succeed each other in time: but this is a mere by-product, a kind of 'side issue' which – and this is a mistake – is studied as an end in itself. Again, 'history will never reveal to us what connections there are, and at what times, between science, art, and morality, between good and evil, religion and the civic virtues . . . What it *will* tell us (and that incorrectly) is where the Huns came from, when they lived, who laid the foundations of their power, etc.' According to his friend Nazariev,

* ibid.

Tolstoy said to him in the winter of 1846: 'History is nothing but a collection of fables and useless trifles, cluttered up with a mass of unnecessary figures and proper names. The death of Igor, the snake which bit Oleg – what is all this but old wives' tales? Who wants to know that Ivan's second marriage, to Temryuk's daughter, occured on 21 August 1562, whereas his fourth, to Anna Alekseevna Koltovskaya, occurred in 1572 . . .?'*

History does not reveal causes; it presents only a blank succession of unexplained events. 'Everything is forced into a standard mould invented by the historians: Tsar Ivan the Terrible, on whom Professor Ivanov is lecturing at the moment, after 1560 suddenly becomes transformed from a wise and virtuous man into a mad and cruel tyrant. How? Why? – You mustn't even ask . . .'† And half a century later, in 1908, he declares to Gusev: 'History would be an excellent thing if only it were true.'‡ The proposition that history could (and should) be made scientific is a commonplace in the

* V. N. Nazariev, 'Lyudi bylogo vremeni', *L. N. Tolstoy v vospominaniyakh sovremennikov* (Moscow, 1955), vol. 1, p. 52.
† ibid., pp. 52–3.
‡ N. N. Gusev, *Dva goda s L. N. Tolstym* (Moscow, 1973), p. 188.

nineteenth century; but the number of those who interpreted the term 'science' as meaning natural science, and then asked themselves whether history could be transformed into a science in this specific sense, is not great. The most uncompromising policy was that of Auguste Comte, who, following his master, Saint-Simon, tried to turn history into sociology, with what fantastic consequences we need not here relate. Karl Marx was perhaps, of all thinkers, the man who took his programme most seriously; and made the bravest, if one of the least successful, attempts to discover general laws which govern historical evolution, conceived on the then alluring analogy of biology and anatomy so triumphantly transformed by Darwin's new evolutionary theories. Like Marx (of whom at the time of writing *War and Peace* he apparently knew nothing) Tolstoy saw clearly that if history was a science, it must be possible to discover and formulate a set of true laws of history which, in conjunction with the data of empirical observation, would make prediction of the future (and 'retrodiction' of the past) as feasible as it had become, say, in geology or astronomy. But he saw more clearly than Marx and his followers that this had, in fact, not been achieved, and said so with his usual dogmatic candour, and reinforced his thesis with arguments designed to show that the prospect of achieving this goal was non-existent; and clinched the matter by observing that the fulfilment of this scientific hope would end human life as we knew it: 'If we allow that human life can be ruled by reason, the possibility of life [i.e. as a spontaneous activity involving consciousness of free will] is destroyed.'*

But what oppressed Tolstoy was not merely the 'unscientific' nature of history – that no matter how scrupulous the technique of historical research might be, no dependable laws could be discovered of the kind required even by the most undeveloped natural sciences. He further thought that he could not justify to himself the apparently arbitrary selection of material, and the no less arbitrary distribution of emphasis, to which all historical writing seemed to be doomed. He complains that while the factors which determine the life of mankind are very various, historians select from them only some single aspect, say the political or the economic, and represent it as primary, as the efficient cause of social change; but then, what of religion, what of 'spiritual' factors, and the many other aspects – a literally countless multiplicity – with which all events are endowed? How can we escape the conclusion that the histories which exist represent what Tolstoy declares

* *War and Peace*, epilogue, part 1, chapter 1.   21

to be 'perhaps only 0.001 per cent of the elements which actually constitute the real history of peoples'? History, as it is normally written, usually represents 'political' – public – events as the most important, while spiritual – 'inner' – events are largely forgotten; yet prima facie it is they – the 'inner' events – that are the most real, the most immediate experience of human beings; they, and only they, are what life, in the last analysis, is made of; hence the routine political historians are talking shallow nonsense.

Throughout the 1850s Tolstoy was obsessed by the desire to write a historical novel, one of his principal aims being to contrast the 'real' texture of life, both of individuals and communities, with the 'unreal' picture presented by historians. Again and again in the pages of *War and Peace* we get a sharp juxtaposition of 'reality' – what 'really' occurred – with the distorting medium through which it will later be presented in the official accounts offered to the public, and indeed be recollected by the actors themselves – the original memories having now been touched up by their own treacherous (inevitably treacherous because automatically rationalising and formalising) minds. Tolstoy is perpetually placing the heroes of *War and Peace* in situations where this becomes particularly evident.

Nikolay Rostov at the battle of Austerlitz sees the

great soldier, Prince Bagration, riding up with his suite towards the village of Schöngraben, whence the enemy is advancing; neither he nor his staff, nor the officers who gallop up to him with messages, nor anyone else is, or can be, aware of what exactly is happening, nor whence, nor why; nor is the chaos of the battle in any way made clearer either in fact or in the minds of the Russian officers by the appearance of Bagration. Nevertheless his arrival puts heart into his subordinates; his courage, his calm, his mere presence create the illusion of which he is himself the first victim, namely, that what is happening is somehow connected with *his* skill, *his* plans, that it is *his* authority that is in some way directing the course of the battle; and this, in its turn, has a marked effect on the general morale around him. The dispatches which will duly be written later will inevitably ascribe every act and event on the Russian side to him and his dispositions; the credit or discredit, the victory or the defeat, will belong to him, although it is clear to everyone that he will have had less to do with the conduct and outcome of the battle than the humble, unknown soldiers who do at least perform whatever actual fighting is done, that is, shoot at each other, wound, kill, advance, retreat and so on.

Prince Andrey, too, knows this, most clearly at Borodino, where he is mortally wounded. He begins to understand the truth earlier, during the period when he is making efforts to meet the 'important' persons who seem to be guiding the destinies of Russia; he then gradually becomes convinced that Alexander's principal adviser, the famous reformer Speransky, and his friends, and indeed Alexander himself, are systematically deluding themselves when they suppose their activities, their words, memoranda, rescripts, resolutions, laws and so forth to be the motive factors which cause historical change and determine the destinies of men and nations; whereas in fact they are nothing: only so much self-important milling in the void. And so Tolstoy arrives at one of his celebrated paradoxes: the higher soldiers or statesmen are in the pyramid of authority, the farther they must be from its base, which consists of those ordinary men and women whose lives are the actual stuff of history; and, consequently, the smaller the effect of the words and acts of such remote personages, despite all their theoretical authority, upon that history.

In a famous passage dealing with the state of Moscow in 1812 Tolstoy observes that from the heroic achievements of Russia after the burning of Moscow one might infer that its inhabitants were absorbed entirely in acts of self-sacrifice – in saving their country or in lamenting its destruction, in heroism, martyrdom, despair – but that in fact this was not so. People were preoccupied by personal interests. Those who went about their ordinary business without feeling heroic emotions or thinking that they were actors upon the well-lighted stage of history were the most useful to their country and community, while those who tried to grasp the general course of events and wanted to take part in history, those who performed acts of incredible self-sacrifice or heroism, and participated in great events, were the most useless.* Worst of all, in Tolstoy's eyes, were those unceasing talkers who accused one another of the kind of thing 'for which no one could in fact have been responsible'; and this because 'nowhere is the commandment not to taste of the fruit of the tree of knowledge so clearly written as in the course of history. Only unconscious activity bears fruit, and the individual who plays a part in historical events never understands their significance. If he attempts to understand them, he is struck with sterility.'† To try to 'understand' anything by rational means is to make sure of failure. Pierre Bezukhov wanders about, 'lost' on the battlefield of Borodino, and looks for something which he imagines as a kind of set piece; a battle as depicted by the

* *War and Peace*, vol. 4, part 1, chapter 4.
† ibid.

historians or the painters. But he finds only the ordinary confusion of individual human beings haphazardly attending to this or that human want.* That, at any rate, is concrete, uncontaminated by theories and abstractions; and Pierre is therefore closer to the truth about the course of events – at least as seen by men – than those who believe them to obey a discoverable set of laws or rules. Pierre sees only a succession of 'accidents' whose origins and consequences are, by and large, untraceable and unpredictable; only loosely strung groups of events forming an ever-varying pattern, following no discernible order. Any claim to perceive patterns susceptible to 'scientific' formulae must be mendacious.

Tolstoy's bitterest taunts, his most corrosive irony, are reserved for those who pose as official specialists in managing human affairs, in this case the Western military theorists, a General Pfuel, or Generals Bennigsen and Paulucci, who are all shown talking equal nonsense at the Council of Drissa, whether they defend a given strategic or tactical theory or oppose it; these men must be impostors, since no theories can possibly fit the immense variety of possible human behaviour, the vast

* On the connection of this with Stendhal's *La Chartreuse de Parme* see *Paul Boyer (1864–1949) chez Tolstoï* (Paris, 1950), p. 40.

multiplicity of minute, undiscoverable causes and effects which form that interplay of men and nature which history purports to record. Those who affect to be able to contract this infinite multiplicity within their 'scientific' laws must be either deliberate charlatans or blind leaders of the blind. The harshest judgement is accordingly reserved for the master theorist himself, the great Napoleon, who acts upon, and has hypnotised others into believing, the assumption that he understands and controls events by his superior intellect, or by flashes of intuition, or by otherwise succeeding in answering correctly the problems posed by history. The greater the claim the greater the lie: Napoleon is consequently the most pitiable, the most contemptible of all the actors in the great tragedy.

This, then, is the great illusion which Tolstoy sets himself to expose: that individuals can, by the use of their own resources, understand and control the course of events. Those who believe this turn out to be dreadfully mistaken. And side by side with these public faces – these hollow men, half self-deluded, half aware of being fraudulent, talking, writing desperately and aimlessly in order to keep up appearances and avoid the bleak truths – side by side with all this elaborate machinery for concealing the spectacle of human impotence and irrelevance and blindness lies the real world, the stream of life which men understand, the attending to the ordinary details of daily existence. When Tolstoy contrasts this real life – the actual, everyday, 'live' experience of individuals – with the panoramic view conjured up by historians, it is clear to him which is real, and which is a coherent, sometimes elegantly contrived, but always fictitious construction. Utterly unlike her as he is in almost every other respect, Tolstoy is, perhaps, the first to propound the celebrated accusation which Virginia Woolf half a century later levelled against the public prophets of her own generation – Shaw and Wells and Arnold Bennett – blind materialists who did not begin to understand what it is that life truly consists of, who mistook its outer accidents, the unimportant aspects which lie outside the individual soul – the so-called social, economic, political realities – for that which alone is genuine, the individual experience, the specific relation of individuals to one another, the colours, smells, tastes, sounds and movements, the jealousies, loves, hatreds, passions, the rare flashes of insight, the transforming moments, the ordinary day-to-day succession of private data which constitute all there is – which are reality.

What, then, is the historian's task? To describe the ultimate data of subjective experience – the personal lives lived by men, the 'thoughts, knowledge, poetry, music, love, friendship, hates, passions' of which, for Tolstoy, 'real' life is compounded, and only that? That was the task to which Turgenev was perpetually calling Tolstoy – him and all writers, but him in particular, because therein lay his true genius, his destiny as a great Russian writer; and this he rejected with violent indignation even during his middle years, before the final religious phase. For this was not to give the answer to the question of what there is, and why and how it comes to be and passes away, but to turn one's back upon it altogether, and stifle one's desire to discover how men live in society, and how they are affected by one another and by their environment, and to what end. This kind of artistic purism – preached in his day by Flaubert – this kind of preoccupation with the analysis and description of the experience and the relationships and problems and inner lives of individuals (later advocated and practised by Gide and the writers he influenced, both in France and in England) struck him as both trivial and false. He had no doubt about his own superlative skill in this very art, or that it was precisely this for which he was admired; and he condemned it absolutely.

In a letter written while he was working on *War and Peace* he said with bitterness that he had no doubt that what the public would like best would be his scenes of social and personal life, his ladies and his gentlemen, with their petty intrigues and entertaining conversations and marvellously described small idiosyncrasies.* But these are the trivial 'flowers' of life, not the 'roots'. Tolstoy's purpose is the discovery of the truth, and therefore he must know what history consists of, and recreate only that. History is plainly not a science, and sociology, which pretends that it is, is a fraud; no genuine laws of history have been discovered, and the concepts in current use – 'cause', 'accident', 'genius' – explain nothing: they are merely thin disguises for ignorance. Why do the events the totality of which we call history occur as they do? Some historians attribute events to the acts of individuals, but this is no answer: for they do not explain how these acts 'cause' the events they are alleged to 'cause' or 'originate'.

There is a passage of savage irony intended by Tolstoy to parody the average school histories of his time, sufficiently typical to be worth reproducing in full:†

---

* Cf. the profession of faith in his celebrated – and militantly moralistic – introduction to an edition of Maupassant whose genius, despite everything, he admires ('Predislovie k sochine-niyam Gyui de Mopassana', op. cit [p. 17 above, first note], vol. 30, pp. 3–24). He thinks much more poorly of Bernard Shaw, whose social rhetoric he calls stale and platitudinous (diary entry for 31 January 1908, ibid., vol. 56, pp. 97–8).

† *War and Peace*, epilogue, part 2, chapter 1.

Louis XIV was a very proud and self-confident man. He had such and such mistresses, and such and such ministers, and he governed France badly. The heirs of Louis XIV were also weak men, and also governed France badly. They also had such and such favourites and such and such mistresses. Besides which, certain persons were at this time writing books. By the end of the eighteenth century there gathered in Paris two dozen or so persons who started saying that all men were free and equal. Because of this in the whole of France people began to slaughter and drown each other. These people killed the king and a good many others. At this time there was a man of genius in France – Napoleon. He conquered everyone everywhere, i.e. killed a great many people because he was a great genius; and, for some reason, he went to kill Africans, and killed them so well, and was so clever and cunning, that, having arrived in France, he ordered everyone to obey him, which they did. Having made himself Emperor he again went to kill masses of people in Italy, Austria and Prussia. And there too he killed a great many. Now in Russia there was the Emperor Alexander, who decided to re-establish order in Europe, and therefore fought wars with Napoleon. But in the year '07 he suddenly made friends with him, and in the year '11 quarrelled with him again, and they both again began to kill a great many people. And Napoleon brought six hundred thousand men to Russia and conquered Moscow. But then he suddenly ran away from Moscow, and then the Emperor Alexander, aided by the advice of Stein and others, united Europe to raise an army against the disturber of her peace. All Napoleon's allies suddenly became his enemies; and this army marched against Napoleon, who had gathered new forces. The allies conquered Napoleon, entered Paris, forced Napoleon to renounce the throne, and sent him to the island of Elba, without, however, depriving him of the title of Emperor, and showing him all respect, in spite of the fact that five years before, and a year after, everyone considered him a brigand and beyond the law. Thereupon Louis XVIII, who until then had been an object of mere ridicule to both Frenchmen and the allies, began to reign. As for Napoleon, after shedding tears before the Old Guard, he gave up his throne, and went into exile. Then astute statesmen and diplomats, in particular Talleyrand, who had managed to sit down before anyone else in the famous armchair* and thereby to extend the fron-

* Empire chairs of a certain shape are to this day called 'Talley-rand armchairs' in Russia.

tiers of France, talked in Vienna, and by means of such talk made peoples happy or unhappy. Suddenly the diplomats and monarchs almost came to blows. They were almost ready to order their troops once again to kill each other; but at this moment Napoleon arrived in France with a battalion, and the French, who hated him, all immediately submitted to him. But this annoyed the allied monarchs very much and they again went to war with the French. And the genius Napoleon was defeated and taken to the island of St Helena, having suddenly been discovered to be an outlaw. Whereupon the exile, parted from his dear ones and his beloved France, died a slow death on a rock, and bequeathed his great deeds to posterity. As for Europe, a reaction occurred there, and all the princes began to treat their peoples badly once again.

Tolstoy continues:

The new history is like a deaf man replying to questions which nobody puts to him . . . the primary question . . . is, what power is it that moves the destinies of peoples? . . . History seems to presuppose that this power can be taken for granted, and is familiar to everyone, but, in spite of every wish to admit that this power is familiar to us, anyone who has read a great many historical works cannot help doubting whether this power, which different historians understand in different ways, is in fact so completely familiar to everyone.

He goes on to say that political historians who write in this way explain nothing; they merely attribute events to the 'power' which important individuals are said to exercise over others, but do not tell us what the term 'power' means: and yet this is the heart of the problem. The problem of historical movement is directly connected with the 'power' exercised by some men over others: but what is 'power'? How does one acquire it? Can it be transferred by one man to another? Surely it is not merely physical strength that is meant? Nor moral strength? Did Napoleon possess either of these?

General, as opposed to national, historians seem to Tolstoy merely to extend this category without elucidating it: instead of one country or nation, many are introduced, but the spectacle of the interplay of mysterious 'forces' makes it no clearer why some men or nations obey others, why wars are made, victories won, why innocent men who believe that murder is wicked kill one another with enthusiasm and pride, and are glorified for so doing; why great movements of human masses occur, sometimes from east to west, sometimes the other way. Tolstoy is particularly irritated by references to the dominant influence of great men or of ideas. Great men, we are told, are typical of the movements of their age: hence study of their characters 'explains' such movements. Do the characters of Diderot or Beaumarchais 'explain' the advance of the West upon the East? Do the letters of Ivan the Terrible to Prince Kurbsky 'explain' Russian expansion westward? But historians of culture do no better, for they merely add as an extra factor something called the 'force' of ideas or of books, although we still have no notion of what is meant by words like 'force'. But why should Napoleon, or Mme de Staël or Baron Stein or Tsar Alexander, or all of these, plus the *Contrat social*, 'cause' Frenchmen to behead or to drown each other? Why is this called an 'explanation'? As for the importance which historians of culture attach to ideas, doubtless all men are liable to exaggerate the importance of their own wares: ideas are the commodity in which intellectuals deal – to a cobbler there's nothing like leather – the professors merely tend to magnify their personal activities into the central 'force' that rules the world. Tolstoy adds that an even deeper darkness is cast upon this subject by political theorists, moralists, metaphysicians. The celebrated notion of the social contract, for example, which some liberals peddle, speaks of the 'vesting' of the wills, in other words the power, of many men in one individual or group of individuals; but what kind of act is this 'vesting'? It may have a legal or ethical significance, it may be relevant to what should be considered as permitted or forbidden, to the world of rights and duties, or of the good and the bad, but as a factual explanation of how a sovereign accumulates enough 'power' – as if it were a commodity – which enables him to effect this or that result, it means nothing. It declares that the conferring of power makes powerful; but this tautology is too unilluminating. What is 'power' and what is 'conferring'? And who confers it and how is such conferring done?* The process seems very different from whatever it is that is discussed by the physical sciences. Conferring is an act, but an unintelligible one; conferring power, acquiring it, using it are not at all like eating or drinking or thinking or walking. We remain in the dark: *obscurum per obscurius.*

After demolishing the jurists and moralists and

---

* One of Tolstoy's Russian critics, M. M. Rubinshtein, referred to above on p. 11, note, says that every science employs *some* unanalysed concepts, to explain which is the business of other sciences; and that 'power' happens to be the unexplained central concept of history. But Tolstoy's point is that no other science can 'explain' it, since it is, as used by historians, a meaningless term, not a concept but nothing at all – *vox nihili.*

political philosophers – among them his beloved Rousseau – Tolstoy applies himself to demolishing the liberal theory of history according to which everything may turn upon what may seem an insignificant accident. Hence the pages in which he obstinately tries to prove that Napoleon knew as little of what actually went on during the battle of Borodino as the lowliest of his soldiers; and that therefore his cold on the eve of it, of which so much was made by the historians, could have made no appreciable difference. With great force he argues that only those orders or decisions issued by the commanders now seem particularly crucial (and are concentrated upon by historians) which happened to coincide with what later actually occurred; whereas a great many other exactly similar, perfectly good orders and decisions, which seemed no less crucial and vital to those who were issuing them at the time, are forgotten because, having been foiled by unfavourable turns of events, they were not, because they could not be, carried out, and for this reason now seem historically unimportant.

After disposing of the heroic theory of history, Tolstoy turns with even greater savagery upon scientific sociology, which claims to have discovered laws of history, but cannot possibly have found any, because the number of causes upon which events turn is too great for human knowledge or calculation. We know too few facts, and we select them at random and in accordance with our subjective inclination. No doubt if we were omniscient we might be able, like Laplace's ideal observer, to plot the course of every drop of which the stream of history consists, but we are, of course, pathetically ignorant, and the areas of our knowledge are incredibly small compared to what is uncharted and (Tolstoy vehemently insists on this) unchartable. Freedom of the will is an illusion which cannot be shaken off, but, as great philosophers have said, it is an illusion nevertheless, and it derives solely from ignorance of true causes. The more we know about the circumstances of an act, the farther away from us the act is in time, the more difficult it is to think away its consequences; the more solidly embedded a fact is in the actual world in which we live, the less we can imagine how things might have turned out if something different had happened. For by now it seems inevitable: to think otherwise would upset too much of our world order. The more closely we relate an act to its context, the less free the actor seems to be, the less responsible for his act, and the less disposed we are to hold him accountable or blameworthy. The fact that we shall never identify all the causes, relate all human acts to the circumstances which condition them, does not imply that they are free, only that we shall never know how they are necessitated.

Tolstoy's central thesis – in some respects not unlike the theory of the inevitable 'self-deception' of the bourgeoisie held by his contemporary Karl Marx, save that what Marx reserves for a class, Tolstoy sees in almost all mankind – is that there is a natural law whereby the lives of human beings no less than that of nature are determined; but that men, unable to face this inexorable process, seek to represent it as a succession of free choices, to fix responsibility for what occurs upon persons endowed by them with heroic virtues or heroic vices, and called by them 'great men'. What are great men? They are ordinary human beings who are ignorant and vain enough to accept responsibility for the life of society, individuals who would rather take the blame for all the cruelties, injustices, disasters justified in their name than recognise their own insignificance and impotence in the cosmic flow which pursues its course irrespective of their wills and ideals. This is the central point of those passages (in which Tolstoy excelled) in which the actual course of events is described, side by side with the absurd, egocentric explanations which persons blown up with the sense of their own importance necessarily give to them; as well as of the wonderful descriptions of moments of illumination in which the truth about the human condition dawns upon those who have the humility to recognise their own unimportance and irrelevance. This is the purpose, too, of those philosophical passages where, in language more ferocious than Spinoza's, but with intentions similar to his, the errors of the pseudo-sciences are exposed.

There is a particularly vivid simile* in which the great man is likened to the ram whom the shepherd is fattening for slaughter. Because the ram duly grows fatter, and perhaps is used as a bell-wether for the rest of the flock, he may easily imagine that he is the leader of the flock, and that the other sheep go where they go solely in obedience to his will. He thinks this and the flock may think it too. Nevertheless the purpose of his selection is not the role he believes himself to play, but slaughter – a purpose conceived by beings whose aims neither he nor the other sheep can fathom. For Tolstoy Napoleon is just such a ram, and so to some degree is Alexander, and indeed all the great men of history. Indeed, as an acute literary historian has pointed out,† Tolstoy sometimes seems almost deliberately to ignore

* *War and Peace*, epilogue, part 1, chapter 2.
† See V. B. Shklovsky, op. cit. (p. 9 above, note), chapters 7–9, and also K. V. Pokrovsky, 'Istochniki romana "Voina i mir"', in Polner and Obninsky, op. cit. (p. 11 above, note).

the historical evidence and more than once consciously distorts the facts in order to bolster up his favourite thesis.

The character of Kutuzov is a case in point. Such heroes as Pierre Bezukhov or Karataev are at least imaginary, and Tolstoy had an undisputed right to endow them with all the attributes he admired – humility, freedom from bureaucratic or scientific or other rationalistic kinds of blindness. But Kutuzov was a real person, and it is all the more instructive to observe the steps by which he transforms him from the sly, elderly, feeble voluptuary, the corrupt and somewhat sycophantic courtier of the early drafts of *War and Peace*, which were based on authentic sources, into the unforgettable symbol of the Russian people in all its simplicity and intuitive wisdom. By the time we reach the celebrated passage – one of the most moving in literature – in which Tolstoy describes the moment when the old man is woken in his camp at Fili to be told that the French army is retreating, we have left the facts behind us, and are in an imaginary realm, a historical and emotional atmosphere for which the evidence is flimsy, but which is artistically indispensable to Tolstoy's design. The final apotheosis of Kutuzov is totally unhistorical, for all Tolstoy's repeated professions of his undeviating devotion to the sacred cause of the truth.

In *War and Peace* Tolstoy treats facts cavalierly when it suits him, because he is above all obsessed by his thesis – the contrast between the universal and all-important but delusive experience of free will, the feeling of responsibility, the values of private life generally, on the one hand; and on the other the reality of inexorable historical determinism, not, indeed, experienced directly, but known to be true on irrefutable theoretical grounds. This corresponds in its turn to a tormenting inner conflict, one of many, in Tolstoy himself, between the two systems of value, the public and the private. On the one hand, if those feelings and immediate experiences upon which the ordinary values of private individuals and historians alike ultimately rest are nothing but a vast illusion, this must, in the name of the truth, be ruthlessly demonstrated, and the values and the explanations which derive from the illusion exposed and discredited. And in a sense Tolstoy does try to do this, particularly when he is philosophising, as in the great public scenes of the novel itself, the battle pieces, the descriptions of the movements of peoples, the metaphysical disquisitions. But, on the other hand, he also does the exact opposite of this, when he contrasts with this panorama of public life the superior value of personal experience, when he contrasts the concrete and multi-coloured reality of individual lives with the pale abstractions of scientists or historians, particularly the latter, 'from Gibbon to Buckle', whom he denounces so harshly for mistaking their own empty categories for real facts. And yet the primacy of these private experiences and relationships and virtues presupposes that vision of life, with its sense of personal responsibility, and belief in freedom and the possibility of spontaneous action, to which the best pages of *War and Peace* are devoted, and which is the very illusion to be exorcised if the truth is to be faced.

This terrible dilemma is never finally resolved. Sometimes, as in the explanation of his intentions which he published before the final part of *War and Peace* had appeared,* Tolstoy vacillates. The individual is 'in some sense' free when he alone is involved: thus, in raising his arm, he is free within physical limits. But once he is involved in relationships with others, he is no longer free, he is part of the inexorable stream. Freedom is real, but it is confined to trivial acts. At other times even this feeble ray of hope is extinguished: Tolstoy declares that he cannot admit even small exceptions to the universal law; causal determinism is either wholly pervasive or it is nothing, and chaos reigns. Men's acts may seem free

---

* 'Neskol'ko slov po povodu knigi: "Voina i mir"', *Russkii arkhiv* 6 (1868), columns 515–28.

of the social nexus, but they are not free, they cannot be free, they are part of it. Science cannot destroy the consciousness of freedom, without which there is no morality and no art, but it can refute it. 'Power' and 'accident' are but names for ignorance of the causal chains, but the chains exist whether we feel them or not. Fortunately we do not; for if we felt their weight, we could scarcely act at all; the loss of the illusion would paralyse the life which is lived on the basis of our happy ignorance. But all is well: for we never shall discover all the causal chains that operate: the number of such causes is infinitely great, the causes themselves infinitely small; historians select an absurdly small portion of them and attribute everything to this arbitrarily chosen tiny section. How would an ideal historical science operate? By using a kind of calculus whereby this 'differential', the infinitesimals – the infinitely small human and non-human actions and events – would be integrated, and in this way the continuum of history would no longer be distorted by being broken up into arbitrary segments.* Tolstoy expresses this notion of calculation by infinitesimals with great lucidity, and with his habitual simple, vivid, precise use of words. Henri Bergson, who made his name with his theory of

* *War and Peace*, vol. 3, part 3, chapter 1.

reality as a flux fragmented artificially by the natural sciences, and thereby distorted and robbed of continuity and life, developed a very similar point at infinitely greater length, less clearly, less plausibly, and with an unnecessary parade of terminology.

It is not a mystical or an intuitionist view of life. Our ignorance of how things happen is not due to some inherent inaccessibility of the first causes, only to their multiplicity, the smallness of the ultimate units, and our own inability to see and hear and remember and record and co-ordinate enough of the available material. Omniscience is in principle possible even to empirical beings, but, of course, in practice unattainable. This alone, and nothing deeper or more interesting, is the source of human megalomania, of all our absurd delusions. Since we are not, in fact, free, but could not live without the conviction that we are, what are we to do? Tolstoy arrives at no clear conclusion, only at the view, in some respect like Burke's, that it is better to realise that we understand what goes on as we do in fact understand it – much as spontaneous, normal, simple people, uncorrupted by theories, not blinded by the dust raised by the scientific authorities, do, in fact, understand life – than to seek to subvert such common-sense beliefs, which at least have the merit of having been tested by long experience, in favour of pseudo-sciences, which, being founded on absurdly inadequate data, are only a snare and a delusion. That is his case against all forms of optimistic rationalism, the natural sciences, liberal theories of progress, German military expertise, French sociology, confident social engineering of all kinds. And this is his reason for inventing a Kutuzov who followed his simple, Russian, untutored instinct, and despised or ignored the German, French and Italian experts; and for raising him to the status of a national hero, which he has, partly as a result of Tolstoy's portrait, retained ever since.

'His figures', said Akhsharumov in 1868, immediately on the appearance of the last part of *War and Peace*, 'are real and not mere pawns in the hands of an unintelligible destiny';* the author's theory, on the other hand, was ingenious but irrelevant. This remained the general view of Russian and, for the most part, foreign literary critics too. The Russian left-wing intellectuals attacked Tolstoy for 'social indifferentism', for disparagement of all noble social impulses as a compound of ignorance and foolish monomania, and an 'aristocratic' cynicism about life as a marsh which cannot be reclaimed; Flaubert and Turgenev, as we have seen, thought the tendency to philosophise unfortunate

* op. cit. (p. 10 above, note).

in itself; the only critic who took the doctrine seriously and tried to provide a rational refutation was the historian Kareev.* Patiently and mildly he pointed out that, fascinating as the contrast between the reality of personal life and the life of the social anthill may be, Tolstoy's conclusions did not follow. True, man is at once an atom living its own conscious life 'for itself', and at the same time the unconscious agent of some historical trend, a relatively insignificant element in the vast whole composed of a very large number of such elements. *War and Peace*, Kareev tells us, 'is a historical poem on the philosophical theme of duality' – 'the two lives lived by men' – and Tolstoy was perfectly right to protest that history is not made to happen by the combination of such obscure entities as the 'power' or 'mental activity' assumed by naïve historians; indeed he was, in Kareev's view, at his best when he denounced the tendency of metaphysically minded writers to attribute causal efficacy to, or idealise, such abstract entities as 'heroes', 'historic forces', 'moral forces', 'nationalism', 'reason' and so on, whereby they simultaneously committed the two deadly sins of inventing non-existent entities to explain concrete events and of giving free

* N. I. Kareev, 'Istoricheskaya filosofiya v "Voine i mire"', *Vestnik evropy*, July 1887, pp. 227–69.

reign to personal, or national, or class, or metaphysical bias.

So far so good, and Tolstoy is judged to have shown deeper insight – 'greater realism' – than most historians. He was right also in demanding that the infinitesimals of history be integrated. But then he himself had done just that by creating the individuals of his novel, who are not trivial precisely to the degree to which, in their characters and actions, they 'summate' countless others, who between them do 'move history'. This *is* the integrating of infinitesimals, not, of course, by scientific, but by 'artistic-psychological' means. Tolstoy was right to abhor abstractions, but this had led him too far, so that he ended by denying not merely that history was a natural science like chemistry – which was correct – but that it was a science at all, an activity with its own proper concepts and generalisations; which, if true, would abolish all history as such. Tolstoy was right to say that the impersonal 'forces' and 'purposes' of the older historians were myths, and dangerously misleading myths, but unless we were allowed to ask what made this or that group of individuals – who, in the end, of course, alone were real – behave thus and thus, without needing first to provide separate psychological analyses of each member of the group and then to 'integrate' them all, we could not think about history or society at all. Yet we did do this, and profitably, and to deny that we could discover a good deal by social observation, historical inference and similar means was, for Kareev, tantamount to denying that we had criteria for distinguishing between historical truth and falsehood which were less or more reliable – and that was surely mere prejudice, fanatical obscurantism.

Kareev declares that it is men, doubtless, who make social forms, but these forms – the ways in which men live – in their turn affect those born into them; individual wills may not be all-powerful, but neither are they totally impotent, and some are more effective than others. Napoleon may not be a demigod, but neither is he a mere epiphenomenon of a process which would have occurred unaltered without him; the 'important people' are less important than they themselves or the more foolish historians may suppose, but neither are they shadows; individuals, besides their intimate inner lives, which alone seem real to Tolstoy, have social purposes, and some among them have strong wills too, and these sometimes transform the lives of communities. Tolstoy's notion of inexorable laws which work themselves out whatever men may think or wish is itself an oppressive myth; laws are only statistical probabilities, at any rate in the social sciences, not hideous and inexorable 'forces' – a concept the darkness of which,

Kareev points out, Tolstoy himself in other contexts exposed with such brilliance and malice, when his opponent seemed to him too naïve or too clever or in the grip of some grotesque metaphysic. But to say that unless men make history they are themselves, particularly the 'great' among them, mere 'labels', because history makes itself, and only the unconscious life of the social hive, the human anthill, has genuine significance or value and 'reality' – what is this but a wholly unhistorical and dogmatic ethical scepticism? Why should we accept it when empirical evidence points elsewhere?

Kareev's objections are very reasonable, the most sensible and clearly formulated of all that ever were urged against Tolstoy's view of history. But in a sense he missed the point. Tolstoy was not primarily engaged in exposing the fallacies of histories based on this or that metaphysical schematism, or those which sought to explain too much in terms of some one chosen element particularly dear to the author (all of which Kareev approves), or in refuting the possibility of an empirical science of sociology (which Kareev thinks unreasonable of him) in order to set up some rival theory of his own. Tolstoy's concern with history derives from a deeper source than abstract interest in historical method or philosophical objections to given types of historical practice. It seems to spring from something more personal, a bitter inner conflict between his actual experience and his beliefs, between his vision of life and his theory of what it, and he himself, ought to be if the vision was to be bearable at all; between the immediate data, which he was too honest and too intelligent to ignore, and the need for an interpretation of them which did not lead to the childish absurdities of all previous views. For the one conviction to which his temperament and his intellect kept him faithful all his life was that all previous attempts at a rational theodicy – to explain how and why what occurred as and when it did, and why it was bad or good that it should or should not do so – all such efforts were grotesque absurdities, shoddy deceptions which one sharp, honest word was sufficient to blow away.

The Russian critic Boris Eikhenbaum, who has written the best critical work on Tolstoy in any language,* in the course of it develops the thesis that what oppressed Tolstoy most was his lack of positive convictions; and that the famous passage in *Anna Karenina* in which Levin's brother tells him that he – Levin – had no positive beliefs, that even communism, with its artificial,

---

* B. M. Eikhenbaum, *Lev Tolstoy* (Leningrad, 1928, 1931), vol. 1, pp. 123–4.

'geometrical', symmetry, is better than total scepticism of his – Levin's – kind, in fact refers to Lev Nikolaevitch himself, and to the attacks on him by his brother Nikolay Nikolaevich. Whether or not the passage is literally autobiographical – and there is little in Tolstoy's writing that, in one way or another, is not – Eikhenbaum's theory seems, in general, valid. Tolstoy was by nature not a visionary; he saw the manifold objects and situations on earth in their full multiplicity; he grasped their individual essences, and what divided them from what they were not, with a clarity to which there is no parallel. Any comforting theory which attempted to collect, relate, 'synthesise', reveal hidden substrata and concealed inner connections, which, though not apparent to the naked eye, nevertheless guaranteed the unity of all things, the fact that they were 'ultimately' parts one of another with no loose ends – the ideal of the seamless whole – all such doctrines he exploded contemptuously and without difficulty. His genius lay in the perception of specific properties, the almost inexpressible individual quality in virtue of which the given object is uniquely different from all others. Nevertheless he longed for a universal explanatory principle; that is, the perception of resemblances or common origins, or single purpose, or unity in the apparent variety of the mutually exclusive bits and pieces which composed the furniture of the world.* Like all very penetrating, very imaginative, very clear-sighted analysts who dissect or pulverise in order to reach the indestructible core, and justify their own annihilating activities (from which they cannot abstain in any case) by the belief that such a core exists, he continued to kill his rivals' rickety constructions with cold contempt, as being unworthy of intelligent men, always hoping that the desperately-sought-for 'real' unity would presently emerge from the destruction of the shams and frauds – the knock-kneed army of eighteenth- and nineteenth-century philosophies of history. And the more obsessive the suspicion that perhaps the quest was vain, that no core and no unifying principle would ever be discovered, the more ferocious the measures to drive this thought away by increasingly merciless and ingenious executions and more and more false claimants to the title of the truth. As Tolstoy moved away from literature to polemical writing this tendency became increasingly prominent: the irritated awareness at the back of his mind that no final solution was ever, in principle, to be

* Here the paradox appears once more, for the 'infinitesimals', whose integration is the task of the ideal historian, must be reasonably uniform to make this operation possible; yet the sense of 'reality' consists in the sense of their unique differences.

found, caused Tolstoy to attack the bogus solutions all the more savagely for the false comfort they offered – and for being an insult to the intelligence.* Tolstoy's purely intellectual genius for this kind of lethal activity was very great and exceptional, and all his life he looked for some edifice strong enough to resist his engines of destruction and his mines and battering-rams; he wished to be stopped by an immovable obstacle, he wished his violent projectiles to be resisted by impregnable fortifications. The eminent reasonableness and tentative methods of Kareev, his mild academic remonstrance, were altogether too unlike the final impenetrable, irreducible, solid bedrock of truth on which alone that secure interpretation of life could be built which all his life he wished to find.

The thin, 'positive' doctrine of historical change in *War and Peace* is all that remains of this despairing search, and it is the immense superiority of Tolstoy's

---

* In our day French existentialists for similar psychological reasons have struck out against all explanations as such because they are a mere drug to still serious questions, short-lived palliatives for wounds which are unbearable but must be borne, above all not denied or 'explained'; for all explaining is explaining away, and that is a denial of the given – the existent – the brute facts.

offensive over his defensive weapons that has always made his philosophy of history – the theory of the minute particles, requiring integration – seem so threadbare and artificial to the average, reasonably critical, moderately sensitive reader of the novel. Hence the tendency of most of those who have written about *War and Peace*, both immediately on its appearance and in later years, to maintain Akhsharumov's thesis that Tolstoy's genius lay in his quality as a writer, a creator of a world more real than life itself; while the theoretical disquisitions, even though Tolstoy himself may have looked upon them as the most important ingredient in the book, in fact threw no light upon either the character or the value of the work itself, or on the creative process by which it was achieved. This anticipated the approach of those psychological critics who maintain that the author himself often scarcely knows the sources of his own activity: that the springs of his genius are invisible to him, the process itself largely unconscious, and his own overt purpose a mere rationalisation in his own mind of the true, but scarcely conscious, motives and methods involved in the act of creation, and consequently often a mere hindrance to those dispassionate students of art and literature who are engaged upon the 'scientific' – naturalistic – analysis of its origins and evolution.

Whatever we may think of the general validity of such an outlook, it is something of a historical irony that Tolstoy should have been treated in this fashion; for it is virtually his own way with the academic historians at whom he mocks with such Voltairian irony. And yet there is much poetic justice in it: for the unequal ratio of critical to constructive elements in his own philosophising seems due to the fact that his sense of reality (a reality which resides in individual persons and their relationships alone) served to explode all the large theories which ignored its findings, but proved insufficient by itself to provide the basis of a more satisfactory general account of the facts. And there is no evidence that Tolstoy himself ever conceived it possible that this was the root of the 'dualism', the failure to reconcile the 'two lives lived by man'.

The unresolved conflict between Tolstoy's belief that the attributes of personal life alone were real and his doctrine that analysis of them is insufficient to explain the course of history (that is, the behaviour of societies) is paralleled, at a profounder and more personal level, by the conflict between, on the one hand, his own gifts both as a writer and as a man and, on the other, his ideals – that which he sometimes believed himself to be, and at all times profoundly believed in, and wished to be.

If we may recall once again our divisions of artists into foxes and hedgehogs: Tolstoy perceived reality in its multiplicity, as a collection of separate entities round and into which he saw with a clarity and penetration scarcely ever equalled, but he believed only in one vast, unitary whole. No author who has ever lived has shown such powers of insight into the variety of life – the differences, the contrasts, the collisions of persons and things and situations, each apprehended in its absolute uniqueness and conveyed with a degree of directness and a precision of concrete imagery to be found in no other writer. No one has ever excelled Tolstoy in expressing the specific flavour, the exact quality of a feeling – the degree of its 'oscillation', the ebb and flow, the minute movements (which Turgenev mocked as a mere trick on his part) – the inner and outer texture and 'feel' of a look, a thought, a pang of sentiment, no less than of a specific situation, of an entire period, of the lives of individuals, families, communities, entire nations. The celebrated lifelikeness of every object and every person in his world derives from this astonishing capacity of presenting every ingredient of it in its fullest individual essence, in all its many dimensions, as it were: never as a mere datum, however vivid, within some stream of consciousness, with blurred edges, an outline, a shadow, an impressionistic representation; nor yet calling for, and dependent on, some process of reasoning in the mind of the reader; but always as a solid object, seen simultaneously from near and far, in natural, unaltering daylight, from all possible angles of vision, set in an absolutely specific context in time and space – an event fully present to the senses or the imagination in all its facets, with every nuance sharply and firmly articulated.

Yet what he believed in was the opposite. He advocated a single embracing vision; he preached not variety but simplicity, not many levels of consciousness but reduction to some single level – in *War and Peace*, to the standard of the good man, the single, spontaneous, open soul: as later to that of the peasants, or of a simple Christian ethic divorced from any complex theology or metaphysic; some simple, quasi-utilitarian criterion, whereby everything is interrelated directly, and all the items can be assessed in terms of one another by some simple measuring-rod. Tolstoy's genius lies in a capacity for marvellously accurate reproduction of the irreproducible, the almost miraculous evocation of the full, untranslatable individuality of the individual, which induces in the reader an acute awareness of the presence of the object itself, and not of a mere description of it, employing for this purpose metaphors which fix the

quality of a particular experience as such, and avoiding

those general terms which relate it to similar instances by ignoring individual differences – the 'oscillations' of feeling – in favour of what is common to them all. But then this same writer pleads for, indeed preaches with great fury, particularly in his last, religious phase, the exact opposite: the necessity of expelling everything that does not submit to some very general, very simple standard: say, what peasants like or dislike, or what the Gospels declare to be good.

This violent contradiction between the data of experience, from which he could not liberate himself, and which, of course, all his life he knew alone to be real, and his deeply metaphysical belief in the existence of a system to which they *must* belong, whether they appear to do so or not, this conflict between instinctive judgement and theoretical conviction – between his gifts and his opinions – mirrors the unresolved conflict between the reality of the moral life, with its sense of responsibility, joys, sorrows, sense of guilt and sense of achievement – all of which is nevertheless illusion – and the laws which govern everything, although we cannot know more than a negligible portion of them – so that all scientists and historians who say that they do know them and are guided by them are lying and deceiving – but which nevertheless alone are real. Beside Tolstoy, Gogol and Dostoevsky, whose abnormality is so often contrasted with Tolstoy's 'sanity', are well-integrated personalities, with a coherent outlook and a single vision. Yet out of this violent conflict grew *War and Peace*: its marvellous solidity should not blind us to the deep cleavage which yawns open whenever Tolstoy remembers, or rather reminds himself – fails to forget – what he is doing, and why.

IV

Tolstoy began with a view of human life and history which contradicted all his knowledge, all his gifts, all his inclinations, and which, in consequence, he could scarcely be said to have embraced in the sense of practising it, either as a writer or as a man. From this, in his old age, he passed into a form of life in which he tried to resolve the glaring contradiction between what he believed about men and events, and what he thought he believed, or ought to believe, by behaving, in the end, as if factual questions of this kind were not the fundamental issues at all, only the trivial preoccupations of an idle, ill-conducted life, while the real questions were quite different. But it was of no use: the Muse cannot be cheated. Tolstoy was the least superficial of men: he could not swim with the tide without being drawn irresistibly beneath the surface to investigate the darker depths below; and he could not avoid seeing what he saw and doubting even that; he could close his eyes but not forget that he was doing so; his appalling, destructive sense of what was false frustrated this final effort at self-deception as it did all the earlier ones; and he died in agony, oppressed by the burden of his intellectual infallibility and his sense of perpetual moral error, the greatest of those who can neither reconcile, nor leave unreconciled, the conflict of what there is with what there ought to be.

Tolstoy's sense of reality was until the end too devastating to be compatible with any moral ideal which he was able to construct out of the fragments into which his intellect shivered the world, and he dedicated all of his vast strength of mind and will to the lifelong denial of this fact. At once insanely proud and filled with self-hatred, omniscient and doubting everything, cold and violently passionate, contemptuous and self-abasing, tormented and detached, surrounded by an adoring family, by devoted followers, by the admiration of the entire civilised world, and yet almost wholly isolated, he is the most tragic of the great writers, a desperate old man, beyond human aid, wandering self-blinded at Colonus.

61